INSIGHTS

IF BOYS NEVER LEARN, MEN WON'T KNOW

QUINCY C. NEWELL

Acclaim for Quincy C. Newell's

INSIGHTS

If boys never learn, men won't know

"A fresh, timely and truly insightful message for our young men." – David Chaney, Professor of Law and Global Leadership Lecturer

"'Insights' is filled with thoughtful ideas that convey messages that will uplift and empower. Although it is written through the lens of a male's perspective, the book has value for anyone looking to live a purpose-driven life." – Gil Robertson IV, Veteran Journalist & Bestselling Author

"Every young man should read this - regardless of race or where they are from. It is a guide to life that gives you real tools to live it from someone who has learned from life and put those tools to work." – Mike Paseornek, Veteran Film Producer and President of Production, Lionsgate Motion Picture Group

"'Insights' is sincere and enriching. Some of the struggles shared reminded myself of being a first generation immigrant, feeling poor and hopeless in this, so-called, land of opportunity. This book offers a hand that holds you through lessons of what positive energy can derive, and to live out our lives with integrity and honor." – Nina Yang Bongiovi, Award Winning Film Producer and Production Partner, Significant Productions

"Quincy C. Newell's words cut through the noise and pierce the heart of the issue: black boys matter. The quality of black and brown lives and the joy of our children are crucial for us to move beyond survival and into places where we can thrive. The world assaults us with digital noise, information clutter and media messages that don't always show young men how to achieve the American Dream, which is too often a nightmare for most of us. This book offers necessary tools to move our lives toward positive change and personal success. Newell's own life experiences and insight offers guidance and a strategy to meet life's challenges for those willing to do the work. It is a must-read." – Rachel Raimist, Ph.D., Associate Professor, University of Alabama

Insights is a work of nonfiction. Some names and identifying details have been changed.

Published in the United States by:

TwentyOne14
1130 S. Flower Street, #214
Los Angeles, CA 90015

www.twentyone14.com

Grateful acknowledgement is made to the following for permission to reprint previously published and copyrighted material:

All definitions by Merriam Webster
Definition of *fear* by Psychology Today and The Free Dictionary
Bible quotes from www.bible.com

Newell, Quincy.
Insights : If boys never learn, men won't know. – 1st ed.
ISBN: 978-0-9985412-0-4
eBook ISBN: 978-0-9985412-1-1

Cover design: XAS Inc./Glassell House | glassellhouse.com
Editing and book design: Kristen Corrects, Inc. | kristencorrects.com

Printed in the United States of America

To my son Taja Newell,
and all other young men working hard to find their place in the
world

CONTENTS

"The ultimate measure of a man is not where he stands in moments of comfort and convenience, but where he stands at times of challenge and controversy."
– Martin Luther King Jr.

FOREWORD
by Keith Clinkscales

For the diligent and driven, success is not only a goal, it is a way of life.

Dr. Martin Luther King Jr., US Representative John Lewis, former President Barack Obama are leaders who have thrived despite severe opposition, ridicule and injustice. Outside of the political sphere, businessmen like Quincy Jones, Bob Johnson, Dick Parsons, and Sean Combs faced similar challenges.

These men are examples of a level of dedication, intelligence, and fortitude that many strive for, but few know how to reach. Quincy Newell provides here the blueprint young African American men need in order to build the strengths necessary to overcome the unique obstacles black men encounter growing up in America. Newell addresses the reality that some of these obstacles don't just threaten to place limitations on career success; they can also be painful limits to accurate and positive self-perceptions and lead to daunting forms of personal intimidation. He provides tools for character development, mental health, personal fitness, strong familial bonds, and building a meaningful, lasting legacy.

Too many black men growing up in America must navigate entrenched socio-economic challenges without the benefit of reliable, proven guidance. I have been blessed with a strong support system via my father and mother. They provided a pathway to opportunities in education, travel, and employment. While my family laid the brick road of my success, it was the mentors in my life who lit the path and provided spotlights in critical moments. My parents, business contacts, colleagues, and even some of my competitors have provided guidance that shaped my life in countless ways.

Although Quincy was not afforded the same support system I benefited from, through his own strong compass and incredible mentors, Quincy has risen to levels of success few achieve. Quincy understands that mentorship for black men is not simply important, it is critical. He has condensed the lessons he would extend to his mentees into a book for young men he doesn't have the opportunity to meet. I hope you all benefit from his leadership as I have benefited from his wisdom and friendship.

"Life's most persistent and urgent question is, what are you doing for others?" A poignant statement by Dr. Martin Luther King Jr. that resonates so clearly today. While you read these chapters, keep in mind that an important part of growing into a leader is understanding that others will come to you, follow you, and depend on you: you must find ways to respond with support and share the benefits of the knowledge you have acquired—much like Quincy has with this book.

Quincy provides guidelines for success in being both a part of your family and your community. He is a living testament that it is vital to nurture your family and extend your reach to positively impact your community. There is nothing in your life that you will face that is more important than your family, including chosen family. They are your foundation and of utmost importance, not just in how you treat them, but more importantly, in how your actions—both mistakes and triumphs—affect them. This is the fuel that makes great men not only great, but also outstanding leaders.

insight

noun in·sight \ˈin-ˌsīt\ : the ability to understand people and situations in a very clear way. : an understanding of the true nature of something

INTRODUCTION

I was born on September 14, 1967 in New Orleans, Louisiana to Sharon Ann Jones. She was eighteen when she gave birth to me. My mother and biological father were high school sweethearts. She was the smart, pretty Creole girl from the seventh ward; he was the high school basketball star from around the way.

During this time in New Orleans, there was intraracial discrimination between Creoles and so-called darker skinned blacks. Louisiana Creole folks are mixed race blacks that descended from the inhabitants of colonial Louisiana during the period of French and Spanish rule. My family's heritage is a mix of French and Spanish Creole, and because of the discrimination prevalent among blacks in Louisiana during this time, in which darker-skinned blacks were treated differently based on the social meanings attached to their skin color (or *colorism* as it was referred to by Alice Walker), my grandfather did not approve of my mother being with my biological father merely because he was a darker-skinned black man—and more importantly, not Creole.

My grandfather was half Italian and half black. His mother, an Italian woman, put him up for adoption because her family did not approve of her birthing a black child—he was viewed as a disgrace to her family name. That knowledge, that *reality* scarred him for life, just like it did many others throughout history. Those scars drove him to find his place in the world by proving that he was better than others. His choice to marry a Creole woman, my grandmother, was deliberate and therefore supported his ideology that the closer one was to being "white" or "European," the better place you held in society. That was racism manifested.

My grandfather was a proud and influential man, and was extremely protective of my mother. He was a musician—a pretty accomplished one at the time— and traveled often with his big band to perform. There would be times he would be gone from home for months. During one of these long travel periods, my mother found out that she was pregnant and, with the support of my grandmother, married my biological father, a black man. My grandfather had no idea this was taking place, so when he returned and found out, he became furious and immediately went to find my mother. He went to her home and forced her to pack her belongings and leave. This all took place while my father was at work. He had no idea that any of this happened. When he came home, he learned that his wife and newborn son were gone. My grandfather vowed to "put him in the ground" if he ever showed his face around our house again. I didn't see my father much at all after that incident. Our bond was broken forever.

I was not even a year old at the time, so I don't have much personal recollection about this incident—only what my mother, my father, and my family told me. But needless to say, despite not remembering anything about that period of my life, the ripple effect of being torn away from my biological father—and as a result, growing up without a constant presence of a father in my house—affected me and lives with me until this day.

My mother was a strong woman, just like her mother. She raised me the best she could and she taught me everything she felt was important for me to know to be successful in life. But as a single mother, with a mother who was also working hard to raise and keep food on the table for her five children, it was hard. There were many things I'm sure she would have done differently if she could, but she did her best with what she had.

My grandfather never truly got over the idea that my mother did not marry a Creole man. Even more, he never got over the fact that her child, his grandchild, was a "mixed breed," as he called me. Ironic, right? As a result, he would often say that I'm not fully part of his family, and he treated me that way. I was that bastard child in his family of "pure Creole blood." Whatever that is. From an early age I was told that somehow I was not good enough—that somehow, because of this destructive and self-hating social and mental construct prevalent at that time, I did not have the skills or the pedigree to live up to my grandfather's high standards.

When I was three, my mother met another man who would ultimately become somewhat of a father figure to me, even though my mother never married him. They were together until I turned twelve years old. He was a young handsome man and an old high school flame, and was on his way to France to play in a professional European basketball league. He asked my mother to come with him, and she did. So, when I was around four years old, my mom and I moved to Europe. We traveled around Europe, first living in Strasbourg, France, and then in Amsterdam. My experience traveling outside the United States was priceless. I was able to see that the world is a big place and that there is much more to life than what I was seeing in the deeply Southern heritage of New Orleans; my experience abroad gave me a very different perspective early on in my life. I credit that time to opening my mind and understanding that not everyone sees the world in the same way…it was my enlightening period.

During my time traveling in Europe, I saw interracial couples, blacks that were not American, and the N-word was not commonly used as it was in America. It was a vastly different experience for me. While living in Strasbourg, I attended a bilingual school, which taught lessons in English and French. I learned about the history of Europe, French culture and I also got to learn about United States history from the perspective of a European…an outsider. I was four years old, at the age of discovery where your heart and mind have not been so polluted and you're open enough to receive new information without any pre-context. I didn't know it at the time, but I was changed. I no longer believed that things were the same everywhere. I didn't believe one person's point of view was law because I saw that life existence—customs and culture—were different in other parts of the world. That led me to question everything and to always understand that a person's point of view is just that: their point of view.

We returned home from Europe when I was seven. As you can imagine, my newfound way of thinking got me into a lot of trouble while I was growing up, especially in the South. I was always questioning, always challenging ideas, and always trying to carve my own path because I believed it was possible. I guess you can call me a rebel or inquisitive but some called me a troublemaker.

I wasn't a great student in high school. Let me rephrase that…I was smart and very capable but did not do well in applying myself academically. I was always getting into trouble—my mom called it being adventurous. I hung out with the "troublemaker" crowds (that's parent speak for "cool kids") and didn't focus on my studies as I should have. This always disappointed my mother because she wanted the best for me, and she knew that I was capable. She believed whole-heartedly that if I applied myself, I could achieve anything I wanted. She tried hard to be a mother and a father figure to me, but she was a single parent and had to work to put food on the table. She couldn't always be there to make sure I was doing the right things. I was left alone quite a bit—a latchkey kid, as they called us—running the streets, getting into things I shouldn't have, finding new ways to add stress to my mom's life…

Not too different from most teenagers, but probably more trouble than she needed.

What made it worse for her, though, was that I was a bright child; I had a higher than average IQ and was deemed "gifted" at an early age. I was placed in advanced classes at every school I attended...but for some reason I wasn't interested. I found it much more exciting running against the grain, pushing back against the system, and charting my own course.

My mother died of pancreatic cancer in 1984, when I was seventeen. She was only thirty-five years old. Her death changed me forever. It scared the shit out of me. This was a really dark period in my life. It shook me to my core. There were points where I thought I wouldn't make it...that I was doomed to end up in prison or dead. I was really at the edge, being self-destructive, surrounding myself with dangerous people, making bad choices that could've altered the trajectory of my life in a terrible way.

I thought she would always be there...my mother was the only person in my corner no matter what. She was my everything, my teacher, my safe haven, my protector, and my shining light...I didn't know what I was going to do without her. But, thankfully she taught me to never give up and always put one foot in front of the other—and if I did that, I would eventually reach my destination. So after some very dark and painful years, with that lesson in my head, and with pain in my heart, I finally took my first step and started walking.

I floated around a bit after my mom died, sleeping on couches at friends' homes, living in various apartments, guest houses, rented rooms. My grandfather and his new wife wouldn't allow me to live at his home with them; I was told that I wasn't welcomed. I had no other immediate family in Los

Angeles at the time so I had to resort to taking charity from friends and taking care of myself the best way I knew how.

Thank God for friends, though, because without their warmth and support I literally would have been relegated to the streets, living in cardboard boxes as a teenager. This period in my life confirmed to me that God is always watching over you and that what you put out in the world truly will come back to you. I say this because the friends that offered their help and their homes did so because of the legacy that my mother left. Because of the person she was to them. You see, she was a bright spirit and a very caring person. Her life existence left ripples in the world that benefited me. Everyone that stepped up, even though they were not my blood relative, did so because of the type of woman my mother was. Her goodwill reflected on me and they honored her memory by honoring me.

I had some tough years but I also had some pretty good ones. The road was difficult—I'm not going to lie—but with the help of some very special people I call my "angels," God's blessings, and a little bit of good fortune, I was able to navigate the road before me and avoid the common pitfalls that so often trap young black men along our journey in life. I could easily have been a statistic: fallen to drugs, gang life, crime, gone to prison, or possibly been killed—all of which were highly probable scenarios for me and other young black men growing up in the 1980s and '90s.

Despite the challenges I faced, I was able to steer clear of any serious trouble, work my way through college, obtained a bachelor's degree, then a master's degree in business, and then navigate my way into law school to pursue a juris doctor degree. I became a father to two beautiful children (Sierra and Taja) and then a stepfather and mentor to two more wonderful souls (Justine and Moses). I made it my mission to be dedicated to fatherhood and committed to supporting my children and my family no matter the costs, challenges, or circumstances. I would do all I could to make sure they did not have to experience the hardship that I did. I have also been blessed with a lovely wife who supports and encourages me no matter what circumstances we face.

I've been blessed with a lucrative and fun career in the entertainment business, first starting in music and then transitioning into film. I've served as a senior executive at industry-leading companies like Rhino Records, Universal Music Group's Vivendi Entertainment, Codeblack Films, and Lionsgate. I have produced over fifteen film and made for TV projects including two of Kevin Hart's breakout stand-up comedy concert films *Laugh At My Pain* and *Let Me Explain* and two critically acclaimed documentary films, one of which was directed by Hollywood legend Robert Townsend and was an official selection of the Sundance Film Festival, *Why We Laugh: Black Comedians on Black Comedy*, and another commissioned by Showtime and executive produced and hosted by the late Joan Rivers, *Why We Laugh: Funny Women*. I have also been nominated for an NAACP award for my role as producer on T.D. Jake's *Woman Thou Art Loosed on The 7th Day*.

It's been an incredible ride thus far; I have been blessed with incredible opportunity and numerous life experiences people only dream about…and I get paid to do it. Further proof that God is always guiding you if you listen. Like they say, you have a plan, but when God sees your plan, He just laughs because there is only one plan—His plan. I like God's plan much better.

All I have been blessed with throughout my journey thus far is due to God's favor and the lessons I've learned along the way. It was often difficult for me to learn those lessons because, you know, I'm a bit of a hard head, but they ultimately sunk in and have served me well in my life.

That brings me to the reason I'm writing this book: I have been blessed. God has been good to my family and me and I have received invaluable life experiences and lessons that helped me to navigate my place in this world. I don't know if I've earned what I have received thus far or if I have just been blessed by God with insights and lessons...*tools*. Either way, they're not mine to keep. I feel that those to which much is given, much is expected. So, I'm taking a step to share whatever insight I have gained with other young men, young black men who may feel that they are alone in this world and may believe that they amount to nothing because their community, their family, society—the world at large—told them so. This book is to any young man who may think he has nothing to offer and is not deserving of the glory that God has waiting for him.

I feel it is important to put something positive into the world, but I also think it's my responsibility to share what I've learned and to break the cycle of dysfunction that preceded me. The lessons I have learned are important; they are simple and complex at the same time. I don't think these lessons can be taught; rather, they have to be experienced. The good thing is that if you are aware that these things exist, you will be better equipped to recognize them when they appear, making you that much better in making crucial decisions that will affect your life for years to come. I call them my *insights*—the lessons that opened my eyes to a different perspective than what is generally presented to us. The world is a tough place, unforgiving at times, especially for young black men. That's why it's important for us to have as many tools in our tool belt as possible, so we can fight through the static and deceptions that the world and society puts forth.

Though it is my desire to offer guidance and insight to young men of color, specifically young black men, I do believe that this information may resonate with and should be used by all young men who may be looking for some guidance. We all generally face the same challenges and we all experience hardship in our lives at one time or another, and if I can be in any way helpful to young men out there who may find themselves in similar circumstances, that is also my desire. Being a black man, however, it is important for me to make sure that I am of service and offer myself as a role model to other young black men, so they can see and follow by example how their lives can be navigated successfully. In no way is it my intent to be exclusionary; rather, I would like to invite anyone who may find these words useful to them, regardless of cultural background and/or race, to read and utilize the information in a way that may help them.

I don't intend this book to be an exhaustive, academic study of any sort but rather a conversation starter, a thought provoker, an easy read that can serve as a nudge to get you moving in the right direction toward leading the life that is rightfully yours. I hope this book will help move some of the static and clutter out of the way so you can see things from a different perspective. I don't claim to be a professor or a prophet; I'm just a blessed man with a story and some information to share.

So, here's my effort to pay it forward….to you…my life insights.

value

noun val·ue \ˈval-(ˌ)yü\ : the amount of money that something is worth. : the price or cost of something. : something that can be bought for a low or fair price. : usefulness or importance

ONE
You Are Valuable No Matter What They Say

The universal view of African Americans portrayed in the media has a tendency to be inherently negative, oppressive, and sometimes demonizing. These views tend to promote a message that we are not worthy, not capable of achieving our greatest dreams, not valuable. All the while the same sources parade fantastical stories in front of us of fame, riches, and success—creating this belief that the world was not meant for us. All this contradiction creates a dichotomy, causing depression, self-doubt, low self-esteem, and in some cases something much worse: moral suicide.

But here's something that's interesting: All this external input, opinions, points of view…means nothing. The secret is knowing that the only thing that matters is what *you* believe, what you know to be true. No one can determine your value but you.

It is important to understand that the collective voice of society is neurotic, and it attempts to impose its perceptions about you, on you. And oftentimes, its perceptions are colored by its own distorted view of the world, filtered through its own biased lens, whether it be insecurities, prejudices, the need to control. When you receive and *accept* these external inputs about who they believe (or want) you to be as factual, you give up control of your true self—your future, your destiny—and put it in the hands of someone else who does not have your core well-being in mind.

The old adage *only the strong survive* exists in our collective psyche as some sort of battle cry...but the phrase is missing one important element: the need to make others weaker so another can be stronger. Correct, the statement presupposes that it's a natural selection, but what it actually does is perpetuates the need to make others weak so there can be another who is dominant. When we understand that external opinions carry no power unless we give it power, we can then realize our own power to determine our own worth. Understand this: We are in control of our own value determination.

We are all born with the capacity, the ability, and the inner strength to pursue and achieve whatever we can imagine for ourselves. Of course, life circumstance sometimes creates obstacles, and the constant barrage of negative external influences can make it more difficult, but it doesn't erase the fact that we inherently possess the necessary tools to operate at the highest levels of life. There is no one better, more superior than another in totality. We are all human beings. We all have special talents, skills that are unique to us. Only the social construct creates the system that identifies these levels of existence and assigns individuals to groups and classes. The societal caste system is merely a social construct, a way to categorize people based on varying criteria created by a person or a group of people, and oftentimes these criteria are set with the intent of benefiting its creator. Thus, the system is intended to weaken one so one can create superiority over another.

No one can tell you that you are unable, incapable, or unworthy. You are valuable; we are born with inherent value that no one outside of you and God sets. If we just understand that we are the ultimate masters of our own destiny and reality, and that our value is already pre-set at its highest level, our life would be dramatically different. I believe we would also look at each other differently; we would understand that each of us has inherent value and that all we have to do is tap into the greatness that lay in each of us. Instead of believing that self-value and self-worth are things that are given to you or created by someone or something outside of ourselves, we would see ourselves in one another.

I was lucky enough to have a mentor preach this to me at an early age: Despite my circumstances, despite being an only child, an orphan, it did not erase the fact that my value exists and that I am the only one who has the privilege of setting the bar of my own personal value. Hearing that in my childhood set my life on a trajectory that led me to the place I am now.

Once this paradigm was set for me, I would begin to ask... *Why can't it be me? Why not? Who said this isn't for me?* Because I was able to see and establish my own value, I refused to accept any other person's opinion about me; rather, I questioned and scrutinized any outside opinion or perception of my value or capability that would attempt to demean or steer me away from opportunities. I would be critical of their view and force them to justify it. I would then assess the situation for myself, my assessment being based on *my* perception of my value, not theirs. I believed that I could do anything if I set my mind to it. I believed that I was capable. If I didn't know how to do it yet, I would learn how…just like everyone else has to. And if a person disagreed, I would demand that they explain to me what supported their conclusion and why.

The idea that you and only you can set your own value is an important concept, and if adopted, could significantly change how you approach your life.

As an example, up until Barack Obama was elected to become President of the United States of America, there was a worldview that a black man could never be elected as president. In fact, there were some who believed they would never see it in their lifetime. Imagine the faith and the self-belief that President Obama must have had in order to believe that he could achieve such a thing despite the rest of the world not believing. The entire world—even those who would wish it not to be true—deep in their hearts believed that it could not happen. With that environment projecting its own point of view, colored by years of racism and oppression, onto society and in particular Barack Obama, he had only the choice to ignore the world's view of what was possible for him and other black men, and set his own personal value and self standards. If he had not been able to do this, he would have fallen into the social construct that was set by the outside world and would have never imagined himself in such a position. But he did, and he is now going down in history as one of America's greatest and most beloved presidents.

This is the power of self-valuation.

EXERCISE I
What Do I Want To Be? What Are My Natural Gifts?

_____

_____

_____

_____

_____

_____

_____

_____

_____

_____

_____

_____

_____

_____

_____

_____

_____

_____

_____

_____

_____

_____

_____

_____

_____

_____

_____

_____

_____

_____

fear

verb \ˈfir\ : to be afraid of (something or someone). : to expect or worry about (something bad or unpleasant). : to be afraid and worried

TWO
Fear Is A Fraud

Did you know that there is no such thing as fear? Really, it doesn't exist. Fear is a name that was created to identify a biological reaction that your body has to certain external and internal stimuli. That's why fear is purely individual. Every person has a different set of "fears" that's personal only to them.

Psychology Today defines fear as *"a vital response to physical and emotional danger—if we didn't feel it, we couldn't protect ourselves from legitimate threats. But often we fear situations that are far from life-or-death, and thus hang back for no good reason. Traumas or bad experiences can trigger a fear response within us that is hard to quell. Yet exposing ourselves to our personal demons is the best way to move past them."*

Interesting, right? Let's look at that again. *"Exposing ourselves to our personal demons is the best way to move past them."* This suggests that we actually have control over our fears, that by "facing" our "personal" demons, we can move past having a fear response to those specific stimuli. Let's look at this further.

Our minds are extremely powerful. We can think ourselves into being scared, even though there is nothing that we should be afraid of. We can just imagine something and evoke the physiological reaction that brings about fear. That's what "personal demons" are, right? This makes up our storage of unpleasant memories, secrets, and insecurities in our subconscious that we haven't yet been able to shed or overcome. These experiences, memories, and secrets are not happening to us right now; they are stored in our minds but have the power to evoke a feeling in us that, for some people, could immobilize them from action.

But the crazy thing is, it's all made up. It's imaginary. It's all in your head. As easy as you can imagine yourself crashing and burning in an interview, or performing poorly in front of a large crowd, you can also imagine yourself nailing the interview or performing at your best, resulting in a rousing standing ovation. And if you had that opposite mental perspective, you would also notice that your physiological reaction would correspond with feelings of excitement and satisfaction. Yes. You have control over what stimuli you place into your psyche, thus invoking the desired physiological reaction. You've heard of self-affirmation, right? Wake up in the morning, look in the mirror, and speak positively to yourself. Re-affirm that you are able, capable. This exercise is equivalent to you programming your psyche, evoking the proper stimuli to get the desired biological response.

This mindset is, in part, what allows successful people to be…well, successful. This way of thinking allows them to take risks without *fear*. They see the success before it happens. They imagine themselves nailing that interview, winning over that large crowd. Instead of visualizing the possible negative outcomes of their given goal or objective, they instead imagine and, most importantly, *believe* that they will be successful. This stimulates and motivates them to pursue their goals with fervor and determination, undeterred by self-doubt. That simple inversion of thinking can determine whether you achieve your goals and find *your* success.

So, given that fear is purely a self-created construct, it is also reasonable to conclude that you also have the ability to control it. Awareness is the key to tapping into this paradigm. In order to control your fears, you have to first be aware that it is in fact possible to control your reaction to these self-inflicted stimuli before you are able to exercise this control. And once you are aware, you must exercise it. Just like going to the gym and working on a particular muscle or movement, you will also have to work on the mechanics of fear control.

When I first started to get a handle on this, I would take the following action: Whenever I came across a situation that would normally create the fear response for me, I would take a step back and ask myself a simple question: *Is this real or is it made up?* To be more specific, I would ask myself if the feeling that I am having is based on something that is actually happening or is it based on something I am imagining *could* happen? That's a key distinction.

For example, if a large dog is standing in front of you barking and foaming at the mouth, that is actually happening. That is real. You will need to figure out what your proper action will be to avoid being hurt in this situation. However, if you're driving along on your way to an interview and you're having negative thoughts about what *could* happen in your interview and your thoughts are invoking the feeling of fear (such as nervousness, sweaty palms, and so on)…that's not real. Nothing has happened. At that moment, you are just driving in your car. It's all in your head. You are only imagining one of the many probable scenarios, except you are choosing the worst-case scenario for yourself. Don't do that to yourself. I mean…if it's all just your imagination, wouldn't it be better if you just imagined the best-case scenario?

When you become adept at making this distinction and identifying this construct, you will be also more adept at exercising your power to change what thoughts arise. Make a practice of thinking self-affirming, positive thoughts when you would otherwise not. Make it a part of your regimen. Every morning tell yourself that you are worthy…say it out loud. Make it a habit to force yourself to think of every situation in the positive context. The more you exercise this muscle, the more it will become the way you think…who you are.

faith

noun \ˈfāth\ : strong belief or trust in someone or something. : belief in the existence of God. : strong religious feelings or beliefs. : a system of religious beliefs.

THREE

God Is With You…Always

What can I say? God is real. Trust me. He is always with you, watching over you. Even when you don't believe, He is there.

My story cannot be told without recognizing God's role in it. I mean, how do you explain my journey? I've been in many situations where I could've gone in the wrong direction…so many times where I was at the point of no return, but yet things always worked out in a way that kept me protected from serious danger. I would love to believe that I'm just that wise and that I've worked hard, and everything I have achieved thus far is due to my hard work and talents. But that's foolish. *Of course* common sense and hard work are contributors, but there are quite a lot of folks out there who are much wiser than I am and that work much harder than I who may not have had the blessings I've had.

So I acknowledge, without pause, that God has had His hand on my shoulder my entire life. In those moments when I could've made a decision that would have changed the course of my life, and those voices came into my head, and my heart opened and my mind expanded...that was God, I know it.

I've acknowledged that my life could have been a statistic. Seventeen-year-old black kid, no mother, no father present, no blood relatives willing to take me in. Homeless, running the streets at the height of the crack epidemic in the 1980s; gang violence at its height with a three-strikes law intended to incarcerate black and brown men at a fast clip. The playing field was not intended for young black men to survive. Yet, strangers—people that were not my family— opened their homes to me and showed me love. I was presented opportunity after opportunity even after making many mistakes; I was spared in situations only God could have intervened in. I was given wisdom by people who would miraculously show up in my life when I most needed them. Therefore, it is important—no, vital—that I recognize the higher power that has been at play in my life. If I do not, that would be a lesson wasted.

If you step back and do your own examination of the circumstances and events in your life, you too may find that there is something else at work. Our society tends to force us to focus on the works of man only. But the truth is that people are merely the vehicles for God's work, and oftentimes when you step back and look at the total picture, how things are connected and come together, you may begin to see a pattern. This pattern may reveal to you that the universe has conspired to force certain events, situations, opportunities, and/or lessons to become present in your life. None of it was by accident…whether it be good or bad. That's God at work.

I implore you to keep your mind, your eyes, and your heart open to the possibility that God may be at work in your life as well. Trust in that idea. Believe that you are worthy of His favor and blessings. Pay attention, search for the signs, and you will also see the work that's going on in your universe. When you are able to acknowledge His existence, you will be able to see the path that He has laid out for you. I wish my eyes were opened much sooner; my journey would have been much easier. But I'm sure that was the point. I needed to go through the things I went through in order to have the foundation to stand on today…and to do this work in God's name, sharing with you, paying it forward.

When you acknowledge God's existence in your life, you learn to look at life a bit differently. You begin to approach life with a sense of gratitude that shifts your paradigm. This allows you to maintain humility within yourself and opens the universe to the possibilities of growth that only occur once you shift from a self-centered mindset to a servant's mindset. When in a servant's mindset, you begin to have a yearning to serve others, to give back, to help make the world a better place. You learn that the true way to fill the holes that may exist in your heart or soul is not through the acquisition of possessions or wealth, but through serving others. There is no more fulfilling experience than being of service to another human being.

You also become infused with *empathy* instead of *apathy*. When we are able to understand what others are going through and open our hearts to the role we all play in nurturing our humanity, you become invigorated. Yes, it's exciting to understand, to *truly* understand that we all have a part to play in our human existence. We are part of an organism that relies on each and every cell, no matter how small or seemingly insignificant, to operate and to thrive. Every cell is important to the organism even though some may want us to believe otherwise.

Search for God in your life. Hold Him close and keep your eyes open. Serve the world around you, be grateful for the little things as well as the big things, and be gracious to others. We are all a part of humanity and we are all responsible for it.

Hebrews 11 1-2 *"The fundamental fact of existence is that this trust in God, this faith, is the firm foundation under everything that makes life worth living. It's our handle on what we can't see. The act of faith is what distinguished our ancestors, set them above the crowd."*

As a man, it is my belief that we should aspire to be a beacon of light for other young men and our family. Through God is the only way to be that beacon. A man who makes it his life mission to walk with God is a man of worth. This doesn't mean that to be a man of God is to be perfect. Rather, a man of God is imperfect and understands that he is imperfect. This knowledge of his imperfections fuels his desire to seek God's wisdom. It allows a man to see, to listen, and to aspire to be a more perfect human being and a servant in the eyes of God. This means we will always be working on improving ourselves.

But be careful: It is easy for us to interpret self-improvement to include material things in its meaning. Instead, we should understand that the improvement we are referring to is all within: your heart, your spirit, your mind, your internal being.

Whenever you have the thought, *I can improve by buying* _____, replace it with *I can improve by being* _____.

No matter the circumstance, no matter how dark it may seem, maintain your faith. Make it a practice to start your day with a passage from the Bible or a quote that derives from Bible teachings. This sets a tone in your mind and sets the trajectory for your day. You'll eventually learn to be strong when you feel like giving up, to be grateful when you're feeling lost or defeated, to be positive when nothing but negativity surrounds you, to be hopeful even when you may have every reason to doubt, to be peaceful when you want to be enraged. When you are constantly filling your spirit with God's words, you will learn that you have the power to never allow these situations to control you—no matter what.

Trust, have faith. Even though you may not see it, you are not on this journey alone.

failure

noun fail·ure \ˈfāl-yər\ 1.) a. : omission of occurrence or performance; *specifically* : a failing to perform a duty or expected action <*failure* to pay the rent on time>. b. (1): a state of inability to perform a normal function <kidney *failure*> — compare heart failure (2): an abrupt cessation of normal functioning <a power *failure*>. c. : a fracturing or giving way under stress <structural *failure*> 2.) a. : lack of success. b. : a failing in business

FOUR

Failure Is a Figment of Your Imagination

There is no such thing as failure. Failure is just a construct that we create to define circumstances that we find ourselves in and the feeling we get as a result of not meeting certain expectations. Failure is simply an event or set of circumstances that fall short of pre-set expectations.

Instead of looking at things under the label of "failure," let's look at things as "experiences" and "learning opportunities." Every time you embark on a goal, a plan, or a mission, you establish a set of expectations, which is what you desire or what you or someone else establishes as a success metric. But truthfully, this is only an expectation set by yourself or a third party. And when you do not achieve or surpass that expectation, the external world labels it as *failing.*

I don't believe that. What I believe is that every circumstance, whether you have surpassed your expectations or not, are all learning opportunities. If we can shift our thinking and realize that every scenario, every situation is an opportunity to learn, then we would be better off and more productive than we are. When we think of failure, we become consumed with the idea of what failure *means* and we sometimes—almost all the time—miss the opportunity to learn. What did we learn from that situation? What are the tweaks we can make to improve? What circumstances existed that created the dynamic for us not to exceed or meet our expectations?

Let's use sports as an analogy. When we watch sports, we understand that every team is working through a season by playing games. Each game is either won or lost. But when a team doesn't win a game, we don't say the team *failed* that game. We simply say they *lost* that game. That specific game is an individual piece of an overall objective: to have more wins than losses at the end of each season.

Let's take it one step further. Whenever a team wins or loses a game, they watch tape to examine what caused their lack of meeting their expectation (to win the game). Sports teams are constantly learning—watching tape, figuring out what they can tweak to improve, get better…cure some of the issues they may have. They also watch tape on other teams, learning how those teams operate so they can adjust their strategy and better match the team next time they play them.

If we employ this logic in our own lives, all we would do is look at each circumstance as exactly that—just a circumstance…a game we play. Either we have exceeded our expectations or we have not met our expectations. Every single time, though, we would be watching tape, learning what we've done that restricted us from exceeding our expectations, or what we were doing right that helped us to exceed our expectations.

Throughout my life, I've been blessed enough to have this concept presented to me at the most unique times. One of those times was right after my mother died. This is going to sound crazy, but hear me out.

The death of my mother was of course a devastating loss. After her passing, I was questioning myself. *Did I somehow cause this? Did I fail her? Why is the world failing me?* My mind was operating under the context of failure. However, someone pulled me aside and said to me, "Look, there is no failure here. There is just a circumstance that you're dealing with—albeit a big one—but nonetheless a circumstance over which you have no control." She then asked me: "What are you going to do with it? How are you going to use it?"

At first when this question was presented to me, I was offended, hurt, and then confused. I was baffled. I struggled with this deeply. All I could say was, "What do you mean how am I going to use it?" The more I sat with it, however, the more I began to understand. How am I going to use this experience? The *experience*. That's what she was talking about.

She was trying to shift my paradigm. She wanted me to step back and look at the situation and then understand that this situation was not about me; rather, it was a circumstance that I was experiencing…impacted by. I first had to understand what the experience was, though. I had to step back from it, which meant that I had to pay attention to how it affected me, how it affected others,, how I felt about it, what I was doing prior to the situation that wasn't working in my life, and how this event ultimately would change my life. This construct helped me to examine myself and my environment in a way that I simply hadn't before. It made me think constructively, rather than remain stuck in the narrow mental construct of failure.

Once I understood this important ideology, I started to apply that philosophy to everything. Why didn't that person call me back? Why wasn't that job offered to me? Everything.

If you shift your paradigm, remove the term *failure* from your vocabulary, and replace it with *circumstance*, *opportunity*, and *learning*, you'll be much better off. Your attitude will change; your outlook will be different.

I mentioned opportunity in the prior paragraph. That's right, *opportunity*. Every scenario or circumstance you find yourself in offers an opportunity, an opportunity to learn, an opportunity to improve.

As a kid growing up without a mother and no father or father figure, I saw no opportunity to be successful, to have a family, or possibly even to survive past the age of twenty-one. This idea, this concept became invaluable. Understanding that you can take these many opportunities where you believe you've failed with things you have no control over— things that are colored by the way other people view you—and flip it on its head to be beneficial to you and fuel you forward is a powerful construct that is entirely in your control.

Remember that your state of mind is important. Do not allow anyone to impose the context of failure on you…because there is no such thing.

Now that we understand that there is no such thing as failure, let's set some of your goals. Identify three long-term goals for yourself. Then identify three short-term goals that will assist you in reaching each long-term goal. Dream big, now…the sky is the limit.

EXERCISE II
My Main Goals

legacy

noun leg·a·cy \ ˈle-gə-sē \ : something (such as property or money) that is received from someone who has died. : something that happened in the past or that comes from someone in the past

FIVE
Legacy

What is a legacy? Webster's dictionary describes *legacy* plainly as property received from someone who has died (I would call that inheritance) or something that happened in the past or that comes from the past. I don't find that definition very compelling or insightful, do you? I describe *legacy* a little differently. I describe it as the ripples that emanate from the choices a person makes during their lifetime.

It's interesting that we generally think about our legacy as what we leave behind—typically property. I understand that these things are tangible, easy to understand and grasp. However, it is much, much more than that. There is an element I identify with that is a bit more focused and purposeful: the establishment of a societal perspective based on your reputation and your actions. This perception has the tendency to impact those closest to you, linked to you in either a positive or negative manner.

It's similar to dropping a rock into still water. It causes a ring of ripples to flow from its center point. Those ripples travel outward and impact things around it. The distance the ripple travels is dependent on the size of the rock dropped in the water.

Similarly, when an earthquake occurs, there is usually a central point of where it happens, called the epicenter. This is the specific point in the earth where the earthquake happens. Despite having a specific, identifiable starting point, an earthquake can be felt for miles around—even though the epicenter of that earthquake is somewhere else. The distance the earthquake can be felt is determined by its size.

This is how I identify legacy. The things that I am doing and the choices I am making in my life today send ripples that will forever impact those around me. The bigger the things or choices I make, the further and deeper the distance those ripples will travel. My children, wife, friends, and generations of family may all be affected by those ripples.

It's for this reason that I believe it is my responsibility as a man, especially a black man, to take legacy seriously. What type of ripples do I want to send to my family? Do I want to send them ripples that are attached to a man who was highly respected in his community...known to have integrity, honor, and respect? Or do I want to send them ripples attached to a man who had none of those qualities?

We all have a responsibility to our families, our children, our loved ones, our community...to ensure that our legacies are protected, kept in tact, improved upon and are held with integrity, humility, strength, and accountability. And that through the cultivation of our reputations, we are to fuel our legacy so our children and our families are positively impacted by it.

One of the things that helped me navigate my life is the positive legacy that my mother left for me. As I mentioned earlier in this book, the reason that some of my mentors and angels extended a hand to me was because of the positive experience and the respect they had for my mother. What she did and how she impacted the people in her life left such a positive impression that they then projected that positivity onto me. Therefore they also treated me in a way that they would have treated her, because of her.

It can work in a number of different ways. For instance, if you have children and you're a person who has done bad things in your life—you've hurt people, lied to people, stolen from people—the odds are more probable than not that the community around you will look at your children through the lens of how they view and perceive you. That doesn't mean they won't have compassion, sympathy or will refuse to be helpful to your children; however, they will look at your children through the lens of how they think of you.

You've heard the saying that the apple doesn't fall far from the tree, right? That construct has a foundation in truth. The truth is not that it is a fact that the apple falling from a bad tree will be bad, it's that everything the bad tree bears will carry with it the stigma of that tree. More simply, it would be expected that, because of the reputation of that "bad tree," it would be more probable than not that your child would have the propensity to be more like the tree they fell from. Because of this admittedly unfair but true social belief system, your children are automatically starting with a burden to change the perception created by your reflection.

The inverse of this idea is true as well. If you are highly respected, viewed by your community as someone with integrity, and you have a reputation of being an honest, hardworking, and honorable individual...it is more probable than not that your children will also benefit from that lens. The people who held this positive and respected view of you would not only project their perceptions of you onto your children; they will also think that your child will have the propensity of being more like you than not—that is, an honest, hardworking, honorable individual.

Because of that reality, whether it is fair or not, we then know that everything we do, however we conduct ourselves and interact with others in our own lives, will have a ripple effect on those attached to us, be it positively or negatively.

We'll go one step further. Say you've committed a heinous crime and you are known in your community as doing such. It is fair to say that your community will react to you in a way that would reflect dissatisfaction and disapproval of that behavior. More realistically, the response to your heinous acts may be hostile and you may be ostracized, in one form or another, from your community. Given this, it is also true that your family will be impacted by your actions and be subject to some of the hostility simply because they are attached to you. Your family may also suffer from your actions; be shunned from society, shunned from the community...even though they have done nothing wrong. They will be impacted by the negative reactions that exist based on how the world has labeled you and sees you. This could ruin opportunities for your family and isolate them from society in a way that can damage them for the rest of their lives.

As men and fathers, we have a responsibility with respect to family legacy. Our duty is to build, protect, uphold, and live our lives in a way that positively impacts and improves upon our family legacy. Of course, all of us (men, women, children) are charged with the responsibility of protecting our family legacies, but the men in the family have a distinct responsibility to do so. As men, everything we do, all the decisions we make, should always have our legacy and the impact on our legacy in mind. If we agree to subscribe to that idea, it will help to shift how we approach our choices and our lives. We will always be thinking about how a decision we are faced with would impact our families, their future, our collective reputation, and our life opportunities as a whole.

We believe that our lives are our own. "This is my life to live, I have no one to answer to but God." Some of this is true—it is your life to live and God is a priority, but you do have something else to answer to: your family, your children, future generations, and your legacy.

Understanding that the decisions we make in our lives are all little epicenters, each of which has ripple effects that travel beyond us, is a powerful realization. This could change your life simply by setting you on a trajectory pointed toward being the best person you can be.

If it is true that our life existence impacts more than just us individually, and that what we do impacts the lives of all the apples that fall from our tree, we then understand that we are living and acting on behalf of a higher purpose. How we live our lives today will have an impact on those connected to our lives, and those connected more closely will have the most impact. This single insight can shift your paradigm to how you think about your life and choices.

As a father and a husband, my choices are simple. Live with honor and integrity or live without it. Knowing what I know now, it's an easy choice. It essentially comes down to the question: *What foundation do I want my legacy to be built upon?* My answer is that I want to be a good man; I want my life to positively impact the apples that fall from my tree.

Coming from a family where my father was absent, my mother died when I was young, where our family legacy was not honored, nurtured, or respected by its patriarch, I made it my mission to change that for my family and break the cycles that need to be broken. I feel that, as a man, a son, a father, it is my job and my *duty* to do so. I owe that to my mother, my children, and my family. Every day that I walk, I carry that with me.

This mindset makes me a better man. It brings clarity to my decision-making, and it brings purpose to my life. I will say again to any young men who have been told that you have no value, you have no purpose...I propose we counter that with the idea and *truth* that your life purpose is established upon your birth. You're here to make a difference, to move your family legacy forward, to bring it closer to God, and to improve upon it in a way that serves God's will. Every small choice you make contributes to that mission. Each choice makes a difference, makes small shifts in the tide of your family's legacy trajectory and lays the groundwork. Each decision you make toward building a positive legacy helps to pour the concrete for the foundation, puts bricks in the wall, and continues to build upon the foundation of your family's legacy.

Sometimes we are burdened with the enormous task of rebuilding. It is possible that your family history may have been impacted by tragedy, misfortune, societal circumstances, and so on. This is a sad truth, more often than not with black Americans and other people of color. There are family legacies that have been disrupted or destroyed by years of racism, oppression, prejudice, and social injustice. That should not stop us, though. The task may be daunting, yes, but not impossible. We simply have to put one foot in front of the other and begin to rebuild the foundation, take the bricks that have been torn apart and broken down and put them in their rightful place. We have to pick each brick up and start to rebuild our foundation.

If you are able to establish that mindset within yourself and push it forward to your family, make it a part of the family psychology, then your family will have a collective purpose. Every person in your family will begin picking up bricks and rebuilding the foundation for your family legacy.

Let's commit together to hold this responsibility dear and preach it to our families. Let's work to build it into our family character so all of our family members walk with a sense of pride and purpose knowing they all have a stake in upholding the legacy for the future of our families.

mentor

noun men·tor \ˈmen-ˌtə̇r, -tər\ : someone who teaches or gives help and advice to a less experienced and often younger person

SIX
Mentorship Is All Around You

Mentorship presents itself in a variety of ways. It's not always what we think it might be, though. When I speak to most young folks, their description of mentorship is a formal arrangement two people have with each other. I'm sure we all have some idea of what mentorship looks like, but the reality is mentorship is around us every day, all day.

You may be in line at your local coffee shop, strike up a conversation with the person behind you, and they share some insightful information. You may be in the elevator with a co-worker and that co-worker gives you a tidbit of useful information you didn't have prior to that exchange. You may be in the audience at a conference listening to a keynote speech. It could be the time you spent with your school counselor, or the message you received from your pastor at church.

Ultimately, mentorship is up to you. Once you change your paradigm about what mentorship actually is, you can receive it every day of your life. The reason you can do this is because you'd be looking for it, seeking it in every interaction you find yourself in because you'd have a different understanding of what mentorship looks like.

Mentorship, from my perspective, is the receipt of enlightening, helpful, and useful information delivered from a third party. The receipt of this information could happen in two minutes, five minutes, or five years.

My kids mentor me regularly. Yes, my kids. What I mean by that is that my kids oftentimes force me to see things from a different perspective, which opens my third eye to ideas and ways of seeing the world that I hadn't yet. Often when I'm having a conversation with them, I believe that I'm teaching them when in fact, *I* am being mentored through my interaction with *them*. Because I've been able to open to the possibility of me learning as well, they ultimately end up mentoring me—opening my eyes, teaching me new things, new insights, new ways to look at the world and my interaction with it.

We should throw away our old, narrow understanding of mentorship and open our lives to mentorship being a way of life.

I say this because mentorship is important. If I did not receive mentorship when I was younger, I would not have received any of the insights that I've been able to share with you in this book. To be frank, most of what I've received in the form of mentorship was from a variety of relationships. Some of these mentorships and lessons were very, very brief. Others lasted for a season. Some I still receive to this day. The important thing was that I understood that mentorship happened everywhere, at all times.

And it is up to us to look for it, to accept it, to receive it. To understand that that's what it is.

In an earlier chapter, I spoke about the importance of learning, looking at your circumstances and learning from the situation so it can be used to improve yourself. Mentorship is the same concept— it's the string that runs through the philosophy of my message in this book, the idea that learning is a constant. It is something that you do all the time, no matter what the situation. And it is something that you should keep your mind open to all the time.

There are times when I'm riding in my car, surveying the road, the other drivers, and watching the traffic flow. I find that I'm always looking for information to help me be a more efficient driver or to keep me from dangerous situations. I also do this when I am traveling; I am always observing, seeking to understand so that I may add new information that may contribute to my understanding of the world around me. My personal mantra is to be observant and always look for and be open to information that contributes to my mental and emotional growth.

It is also important to understand that in order to receive, you also have to be willing to give. Approach mentorship with humility and a willingness to reciprocate. Do not approach mentorship selfishly with the other person solely viewed as a source. If you have no interest in being of service through mentorship, it becomes very robotic, very self-serving. Mentorship is a reciprocal thing. Remember that mentors, though they want to give and share, also believe it's fulfilling because of what they receive from it. It's helpful to understand that as much as you are seeking mentorship, you are also fulfilling another person's desire to be of service. That's the construct where mentorship is the most fruitful, because nobody wants to be in a relationship where the other person is solely after what they can get from you.

It's a refreshing, invigorating mental space to be in when you're constantly looking for opportunities to learn and be of service. You know there is a saying: *Listen more than you speak*. Well, really what that means to me is *be of service*. Serve and you shall receive learning tenfold.

complete

adjective com·plete \ kəm-ˈplēt\ : having all necessary parts. : not lacking anything. : not limited in any way. : not requiring more work. : entirely done or completed

SEVEN
The Completion Mindset

You always hear people saying that you can do whatever you want to do as long as you work hard at it. That's true, but it doesn't mean that you will be successful at it or should I say, meet your highest expectations or be a millionaire. What it *does* mean is that if you set your mind to something, you can actually do it. This brings up the idea of completion. My mother taught me that you should always finish what you set out to do.

Using this context, you can then say if you take the steps and exert the appropriate amount of energy and time to become qualified enough to do or be a particular thing—like an engineer, a teacher, a lawyer—you can do it. This, of course, is if you put in the necessary work to meet the required criteria and you take the steps to acquire the skill and tools to complete the task.

If you want to do something and you are determined to do it, start it and complete it. Don't stop. Don't quit in the middle just because it's possible that you may not achieve your own expectations. If you plan to start something and have already taken the first step, you might as well finish.

Now, people will say, "What if it's not going to work?" or "What if it's evident that I'm not going to achieve what I set out to achieve—won't I just be wasting my time?" That's a different issue. That question is about the quality of your choices. I'm talking about the idea that we should be better at choosing what we want to start. It's also true that you should never start something that you do not intend to finish…and you should never start something that you *really* don't want. Not only would you be wasting your own time, you would be wasting the time of others offering to help you achieve your stated goal.

Let's start by separating the two ideas: 1) Complete what you start, and 2) Be more selective and more strategic about what you choose to pursue. Make sense?

It's really an easy concept. All we are doing is breaking it down to address these parts separately and clearly. My mother explained this to me when I was young because I would always start something, like building a model car, then I would lose interest and quit. This would make my mother angry because I would make her spend her hard-earned money to buy the model for me only for me to quit before I finished it. To her, it was deeply offensive and inconsiderate of me to waste her money that way. So she set out to teach me the differences between those two things, but she also taught me the importance of completion: Once you have decided to start something, you've evaluated it properly, you decide it is worth your time and the end result is something you would like to see come to fruition, and you are prepared to accept the end result in whatever form it manifests, be respectful to yourself and to those supporting you in your endeavor by making sure that you complete it.

Completion also does another important thing for you: it builds confidence and it builds muscle. (Well, not exactly physical muscle, but the *habit* of finishing.) The more you get in the exercise of finishing what you start, the more you build the competence of seeing how to finish. How to complete something. Everything is made up of steps to get from point A to point Z, and when you become adept at identifying those paths to completion and build your muscles with the process of repetition (execution, work ethic, finally completion) you become better, you become stronger. That's a critical thing to understand.

Now that you have made yourself accountable to completing, the byproduct is that you begin to look at your options more closely; you scrutinize them a bit more carefully. Why? You don't want to waste your time—remember, once you start, no matter what happens, you have to complete it. That's your discipline, the standard that you have set for yourself.

Your new standard forces you to evaluate everything in your life through a different lens; you'll begin to make a habit of determining whether or not you really want to do it and assess whether or not you have the appropriate tools to achieve it. This applies to a relationship, a job, a project...*everything*. You will scrutinize them all a little more because you have set a standard for yourself to which you hold yourself accountable.

Completion also does something for your legacy—remember, we talked about legacy being important. Being a respectful, honorable, accountable human being in the eyes of your family, friends, co-workers, and your community. Completion helps lend credibility to that. You are a person, man or woman, of their word. If you say you are going to do something, people know that you will do it. You don't haphazardly commit yourself to things that you don't intend to finish.

That's pretty powerful if you think about it. If you look at how you want the outside world to view you, and you've determined the level of importance your legacy will have in your life, you'll realize the importance of completion and how that lends to building a legacy for yourself. If a person knows they can count on you to deliver when you say you will, you will receive something invaluable in return: respect and trustworthiness. That respect and trustworthiness will be extended to your family through your legacy.

manhood

noun man·hood \ˈman-ˌhud\ : the qualities (such as strength and courage) that are expected in a man. : the state or condition of being an adult man and no longer a boy. : adult men

EIGHT
The Four Pillars Of Manhood

In today's society, being a "man" is very different than what it was during my grandfather's generation. During that era, men were expected to be tough, masculine, emotionless, breadwinners...the undisputed heads of the family. Today, the definition of men includes things that have been traditionally reserved as feminine attributes, like being sensitive, nurturing, a hands-on-parent, emotionally vulnerable...not that those things are bad for men to embrace, it just wasn't how society defined men in the past. Men were expected to work hard, have a career, take care of their families, be the pillar of strength in their homes, and protect their loved ones at all costs. Any sense of vulnerability or sensitivity was viewed as weakness among men. However, if you ask young men today if they think that being nurturing, caring, and a good and attentive dad is considered being weak, they would most likely say no—in fact, they would most likely say that it is those attributes that defines what being a man is all about.

Many people believe that today's man has lost his way. Though it is a positive progression to expand our emotional capacity and redefine our roles as men in our families, there is a belief that we have begun to lose touch with what is central to manhood. Some are calling for a reawakening of the masculine spirit among today's men. There are many programs and events that target men promoting this idea, and encourage men to reexamine their roles by exploring their inner psyche and challenging the definitions that today's society has placed on them. The goal, I believe, is to reconnect men with the core character of manhood while attempting to resolve the conflict between modern society's expectations and our ancient masculine biological and emotional foundation.

To achieve a healthy balance of the past and the present, men must be able to define their lives and the order of their priorities. I boil that down to being able to identify and discover our purpose in life. I believe that discovering purpose in one's life is a personal journey that can make the difference between emptiness and ultimate satisfaction.

My purpose, as I mentioned earlier, is to continue to build a legacy, a foundation for my family to stand upon and to share with the world the lessons and insights I have gained along the way. My hope is that they too can navigate this world and complete their missions of purpose.

In the chapter where I discussed legacy, I proposed that our life purpose is established upon our birth, that we're here to move our family legacies forward, to bring our legacy closer to God and to improve upon it in a way that serves God's will. That is a truth I hold self-evident.

All this talk about what it means to be a man made me notice something. Not once did I mention words like *honor*, *integrity*, or *loyalty*. The dictionary definition of manhood doesn't use any of those words in its definition either, nor does it use the word *God*. Why? Are we thinking about manhood all wrong? Are we trying to identify ourselves as it relates to our physical manifestations within a societal construct rather than defining manhood through our psychological and spiritual paradigms?

To define manhood, you must first define the elements that make up a man's psychology. If we can identify which attributes define a man's psychology, I believe we would learn to better understand and shape the human nature of men rather than project on men our ideas shaped by historical or current social and environmental trends.

Henry Ward Beecher once said, "A man's achievements do not tell us what he is or what he is worth. It's what lies inside the man, not what he holds or wears that will tell you who he is and what he is worth." This is a powerful statement, don't you think? Basically, this is telling us that it doesn't matter how much money or how many possessions a man has. You will never know his true value or who he is until you know what he believes and what his standards are. I think that is spot on.

What standards *do* men live by today? If we can establish what standards we should live by as men, we can then identify *how* we live and ultimately shape *who* we are as men. And if we can identify which attributes serve men and society in a way that helps to push society positively and constructively forward, we can also narrow down which attributes should be part of being a man.

With that mission in mind, I've worked to identify attributes I believe to be central to my manhood to define what being a man is—or should be—all about. This is the psychology that helps to keep your heart, spirit, and mind pointed in the right direction. I call these my four pillars of manhood. Identifying and establishing these standards and making them part of my psychology behind living my life has helped me to construct a path with clear markers that help to keep me within my chosen lane—like the bumps in the road that let you know when you've moved too far outside of your lane, reminding you to straighten out. They're there to protect you; they are safeguards to make sure you don't veer off your chosen path.

It is my belief that this approach is a better way to establish a direction for defining your own manhood. Below are the pillars I've constructed for myself, those that help me to walk in the path that I've chosen to serve my life purpose and my legacy.

PILLAR ONE – HONOR

Live your life with honor. Be a man of God. Be a leader, not by force but with humility and service in your heart. Seek to be respected and give respect where it is due. You are the king of your domain, but be a king who lives in service to those who look to you. Be a man your family can be proud of. Be a teacher to those around you. Become competently skilled at something and pass it on. Pay it forward.

PILLAR TWO – INTEGRITY

Operate your life with integrity. Have standards that are in alignment with your legacy quest. Stand for what you believe in, but don't be too rigid to learn. Honesty is important—be a man of your word. Stand up straight and represent yourself with respect. Be a warrior in all sense of the word—for your family, your happiness, your career, and your standards. Be optimistic and share that passion with those around you. Take care of yourself; stay healthy so you can be there for others. You are your legacy…be it.

PILLAR THREE – LOYALTY

Loyalty doesn't mean that you are a follower. Loyalty is an honorable trait. Loyalty is accountability. Loyalty means that you stand solid in your decisions and that you follow through. You know what you want and how to complete. Be loyal to your family, your friends, your God. Be a mentor and show someone else what loyalty looks like. Loyalty breeds security and safety in others, and as a byproduct you will be safe and secure. Loyalty is knowing you can count on someone. Be that someone—show up for those you love and who deserve you.

PILLAR FOUR – COURAGE

Fear is a fraud. Inner strength and fortitude is much more powerful than physical strength. Be a warrior for your family. Protect them and what they stand for regardless of if it is what you believe. Protect your legacy with everything you have. Do not be afraid to stand in your beliefs even when you are the only one who does. Don't be afraid of anything or anyone, but be wise. Stand out from the crowd. Believe.

By establishing these guideposts for my life, I have been able to focus my purpose as a man while bolstering my confidence. By adopting these attributes, I have begun to gain others' respect with the knowledge that I am prepared to act competently, honorably, and without hesitation in my life to uphold the standards I have set and in pursuit of my legacy.

I encourage you to take the time to do a bit of self-evaluation and discovery. Determine what your personal standards are and how they align with your life's purpose. You can then establish your own benchmarks to help you "stay in your lane" and keep focused on walking in the way that supports the building of your legacy.

On the following page, I've added a grid so that you can create your own pillar list. This will help you to start to develop your own guideposts for your life.

EXERCISE III
My Personal Pillar List

Each pillar should contain your standards that align with that pillar. For instance, one of my pillars is integrity. Under that pillar I have included standards such as *live my life with integrity*, *stand for what I believe in*, and *be a man of my word*. Build your pillar list to reflect the man you would like to be and the pillars you want to guide your life.

Pillar I: _____
Pillar Standards:

_____

_____

_____

_____

_____

_____

_____

_____

_____

Pillar II: _____
Pillar Standards:

_____

_____

_____

_____

_____

_____

_____

_____

Pillar III: _____
Pillar Standards:

_____

_____

_____

_____

_____

_____

_____

_____

_____

Pillar IV: _____
Pillar Standards:

_____

_____

_____

_____

_____

_____

_____

_____

_____

CONCLUSION
Listen With Your Heart: The Lessons of Insights

Before we move on, I'd like to express my sincerest gratitude to you for taking the time to read this book. I understand that you have many other things you could be doing, but you took the time to invest yourself in reading what I had to offer. My simple mission is to share what I've learned with the hopes that someone may be able to use it for their benefit. I truly believe it's all of our responsibilities to pay it forward. We are all part of this system called life. We exist together, not apart. Similar to the earth's eco-system, our human eco-system relies on each and every one of us to contribute something, whether it be small or large, to help our eco-system prosper and grow. This book is my humble contribution.

Throughout these pages, we have discussed many things: the importance of believing in yourself and in God, understanding how to complete things as a form of exercise and developing a habit of critical selection, recognizing the importance of your legacy and your responsibility to it, learning how fear is nothing but a figment of your imagination, and comprehending how *failure* should be removed from your vocabulary. I also shared with you my four pillars of manhood. My hope is that these insights may be useful to you and can help you to navigate your life in a way that positively affects you and those with whom you come into contact.

To take advantage of these insights, have an open heart and a determined mind. Be deliberate in your pursuit of your objectives and goals. These things operating together will allow you to receive the information and then apply the lessons with purpose and focus. Just like anything, we first have to get out of our own way to move forward. What does "get out of our own way" mean? It means that we often have pre-formed views shaped by the external input (from other people, or other things) like the articles on the Internet, or views and perspectives of friends and colleagues. Oftentimes we allow these things to form our worldview and our self-view. When we form our viewpoint on others' opinions of us, we give up our ability to think independently and critically, blindly accepting the views of outside sources without first fact checking or testing against our personal and spiritual values. Some call this phenomenon "groupthink." We surrender our power, adopting the group's views and opinions regardless of whether the perspective is right or wrong. Oftentimes, this is done out of convenience; sometimes this is done out of a fear of having an opinion that opposes the "popular view." This viewpoint is not yours and in most cases may not serve your purpose or your moral code.

Be independent and think critically. Stand in your own shoes. That's true strength—the ability and courage to stand apart from the crowd if it's the right thing to do.

Regardless of what you may or may not have learned here, you already have all the tools to succeed in your life. You are born with them. The only thing you have to figure out is how to access these tools and sharpen them. Have faith in yourself and your ability to achieve everything you aspire to achieve. Believe you can and you will.

With humility and appreciation, Quincy.

DEDICATION TO MY MOTHER
AND MY ANGELS

Sharon Ann Jones was born in the seventh ward of New Orleans to a family with a rich Creole legacy. She was the second oldest in a brood of five, but the undisputed leader of the siblings. She was an incredible woman. Beautiful, smart, well read, strong willed. She lit up a room when she walked in. She had that kind of energy that drew people to her…strangers would walk up to her to ask if she was famous.

Everyone wanted to be her friend. It was because of her that I got to see the world at an early age. She raised me as a single mother for most of our time together. She taught me the importance of being a lifelong student, the value of friendship and loyalty, that God and family are my top priorities, and how to be determined. She taught me that my character and reputation are to be protected at all costs…not for my own sake, but for my family's.

She believed in establishing a strong and proud legacy. She did for me. She believed in being honorable. She followed this old school code that doesn't seem to exist anymore.

She loved to dance, read, travel, explore. She was a huge music fan. I would wake up every Saturday morning to the sound of music throughout the house and the smell of food (she could cook her butt off, too). She had an incredible vinyl collection. She would collect concert tickets—she had a shoebox filled with them. She turned me on to Jimi Hendrix, Bob Marley, The Rolling Stones, Sly and The Family Stone, Parliament Funkadelic, Marvin Gaye, Mile Davis, and The Beatles. She was a proud Woodstock '69 alumnus. She was the one who encouraged me to pursue my lifelong passion of surfing.

I live every day to make her proud, to carry on her legacy, to become the man she always knew I could be, and she fought to her very last breath to give me opportunities. She believed in me. Her belief was unwavering, no matter how much trouble I got myself into (and I got into *a lot* when I was a young buck). She never let it deter her quest to help me improve, learn, be better. She had a way of turning things into grand life lessons that forced me to see things in a new light...that left me inspired. She once told me that she secretly admired my adventurous and independent spirit, my willingness to question everything, and my desire to forge my own path, to be a rebel. She did it so lovingly and sincerely, you know? ...Then she spanked me and sent me to my room.

Not too many people in my life now knew my mother. Unfortunately, that includes my children. If they did, they would stand a bit taller today. That's the type of person she was—everyone who crossed her path was built up. She was special. Really...she was special, one of those people that others talk about long after they are gone. I am blessed to be her son.

She taught me to be a warrior, a fighter. To stand by my beliefs and to be my own man...to be proud but not too proud to be humble. She taught me to listen more than I talk, to work hard, and to finish what I start. I have learned from her how to be a good friend, father, husband (still working on those), to be generous, and to pay it forward when I can. She taught me to strive to always set a positive example, and that doing the right thing isn't always the easiest thing, but it will always be the best thing.

These are lessons that stick with me today…and I work to pass these on to my loved ones…really, to anyone who will listen. I pray that I'm doing a decent job. Regardless, I will continue to work at it.

My mother passed away of pancreatic cancer. She was far too young. A little bit of me died along with her…and it cannot be replaced. Funny thing is, I don't want it to. I miss her and I love her. But I want her to know that our legacy is in good hands. I got this.

I'd also like to take a moment and acknowledge my Earth angels. I simply would not be the person I am today if it were not for these wonderful and beautiful human beings.

First, Mike Campbell's mother Judy Campbell, who gave me a warm bed and a roof over my head after my mother passed away. It was a tough time and her compassion gave me strength.

Gaynell Marrero, my mom's best friend from childhood. My mother asked her to look after me and she has stayed vigilant until this day in every way. My roots are strong because of her.

Lisa Turner, another of my mother's friends and cousin once removed. She would drive wherever I was and made sure I was okay, had food…whatever. She also encouraged me to go to school and follow through.

My mother's younger brother and sister— Deborah Jones and Ronald Jones—who would call me to pray and encourage me. Send me money when I needed it. Fly out to visit me just to look into my eyes and make sure I was alright. They were unwavering in their belief in me…they would never let my spirits get down. A very wise woman, and an honorable man. These two God-fearing people shaped my character.

Alicia Krynsky, who was always so kind and warm. She would make sure I was fed and always kept a place for me to sleep if I ever needed it. Compassion and love oozed out of her.

Moza Yontov. One of the strongest women…no, person I've ever met. She always kept an open door for me, no judgment, no questions. She showed me what family really means, what perseverance is, and what loyalty looks like. She made sure I felt like one of her own. Gave me shelter, nourishment, encouragement, and honesty. No filter honesty, the kind that family gives.

And last but not least, my beautiful wife Karina Quezada-Newell. She fought hard for me and for us. She loves me with no conditions; she sees things in me that I sometimes don't see. She often makes me ask, "Who are you talking about?" when she describes the man she sees in me. She's helped to make me and our children warriors, to stand strong with our backs straight, with honor. I love her fully.

These are the angels God and my mother have sent to assist me in my journey. And I appreciate, respect, love, and honor each of them with every part of my being. I thank them all for caring enough to be there. I am because they are. So yes, angels are for real. Recognize yours and don't doubt it for a second.

ABOUT QUINCY C. NEWELL

Quincy C. Newell is a twenty-five-year veteran of the entertainment business and has worked for organizations such as Paramount Home Entertainment, Universal Music Group, and Rhino Entertainment. He currently serves as the executive vice president and general manager of Codeblack Films, a Lionsgate company. He is also a film and documentary producer and a social activist. He loves to surf, is a recreational triathlete, and is a husband and dad to four great kids. He has a passion for mentorship and can often be found with his nose in some sort of how-to book on the weekends. Newell holds an MBA from Pepperdine University's Graziadio School of Business and Management and a Juris Doctor degree from the University of West Los Angeles School of Law. He currently lives in Los Angeles with his wife and four children.

ABOUT KEITH CLINKSCALES

Keith Clinkscales is a media executive and magazine publishing entrepreneur. Mr. Clinkscales has been nominated twice for an Emmy Award and is a two-time Peabody Award Winner. He is also a two-time recipient of the National Association of Black Journalists (NABJ) Excellence in Journalism Award and has been listed among the 2014 CableFAX 100 as an industry power player.

Mr. Clinkscales co-founded Urban Profile magazine in 1988 and sold the publication to Career Communications Group in 1992. Since then, Mr. Clinkscales has served as the CEO of *REVOLT MEDIA & TV*, president and CEO of *VIBE MAGAZINE*, founded by Quincy Jones, and as a senior vice president at *ESPN* where he was responsible for creating the award-winning and critically acclaimed sports documentary series *30 for 30*.Mr. Clinkscales earned an MBA from Harvard Business School and a BS in accounting and finance from Florida A&M University. Clinkscales currently serves on advisory boards for Howard University School of Communications, MillerCoors, and PepsiCo.